Affiliate Marketing

The Beginner's Step By Step Guide To Making
Money Online With Affiliate Marketing

Kevin Ulaner

Table of Contents

Introduction

I want to thank you for having interest in my book, *"Affiliate Marketing – The Beginner's Step By Step Guide To Making Money Online With Affiliate Marketing"*.

This book contains proven steps and strategies on how to start an affiliate marketing business.

Affiliate marketing offers you a chance to start an online business with minimal capital. If you implement it successfully, you may add a few thousand dollars in your monthly income.

This book provides you with all the tips and strategies you need to start your business. It provides you with the fundamental skills and knowledge needed in Internet marketing. It also teaches you the process on how to become an affiliate marketer and how to make your business a success.

Read this book and start building your passive income empire today.

Thanks again for grabbing a copy of this book, I hope you enjoy it!

Chapter 1 – Affiliate Marketing Definition

Let's begin our discussion with what affiliate marketing really is. In the chapter that follows, we will discuss how the affiliate marketing business works for all parties involved.

What is affiliate marketing?

Affiliate marketing is a product promotion style of companies offering their products online. The ultimate goal of this product promotion method is to make more sales. It allows the seller company to reach market segments that it would not normally reach using its own marketing resources.

In this process, the company encourages influential marketers around the Internet to promote their products or services. These marketers are given a unique affiliate link by each prospective company that they can share to the people they could influence. The normal everyday users who click on these links will be directed to the webpage of the given company's product or service. If for example I clicked on one of these links a cookie would be stored on my computer with the marketer's information. In this way each company can track which links get clicked by visitors and can then give credit to the marketer. If the visitor decides to buy a product, the marketer gets a commission of the sale. These cookies are typically tracked and active for roughly 30 days. So if someone had clicked on your link but didn't make a purchase just yet this is ok because should they visit the same site again you would still get credit for the sale.

In this process, there are three stakeholders, the seller, the marketer and the buyer. Affiliate marketing provides a platform wherein all participants come out as winners. By buying from an affiliate marketer, the buyers get to learn about the product in detail before they are committed to a purchase. This gives the buyer a reputable source of pre-purchase information. In the process, they are more likely to make informed decisions and avoid buying bad products.

At the same time, the company also gains something. For one, they get a sale that they normally would not have gotten without the efforts of the internet marketer. Without affiliate marketing, the seller would not have reached the market segment of the buyer. They also would not have gained the trust of the buyer that facilitated the purchase. If their product or service meets the expectations of the buyer, they could turn one-time buyers into loyal customers.

Lastly, the affiliate marketer gets a commission that is usually equal to a percentage of the sale. This is his or her reward for successfully facilitating a sale. In many ways, the affiliate marketer acts like an online salesperson. He finds products and services and promotes them to the right people.

How much do you earn from each sale?

The amount of commission that the marketers get depends on the terms and conditions of the affiliate program. If you want to be a part of a program, check this information first.

The lower end commissions usually hover around 4-6%. However, some companies offer much higher commission rates. Some programs also adjust their commission rates based on the performance of the affiliate. If the affiliate is a beginner, the program may start out at 8%. As he sells more products in the month, the rate may also increase. The Amazon Associates affiliate network works in a similar way.

Professional affiliate marketers with long email lists and millions of traffic in their website could email the company directly and ask if they can get a higher commission rate. If you have authority in your niche and you think you can convince the seller company to give you a higher rate, you should also contact them.

How much will you earn from this form of business?

Your earnings in this form of business will depend on your ability to make online sales. However, you could start earning even if you still do not have a business system in mind by telling your friends and family to buy using your affiliate link.

Let's say you are already an Amazon Associates' member and you know a lot of people who are already buying from the website. You should send them your link. Explain to them the situation and ask them to help you out. While talking to them, emphasize that using your link to make their purchase does not add any cost to their purchases.

While this method will not add a significant amount to your business, it will help boost your sales numbers to raise your commission rates.

The bulk of the potential income, however, comes from your online marketing efforts. Most people just place their affiliate links around the Internet, hoping that people will click on them. This strategy or lack there of is not very effective at all. It will also get you banned if the websites moderators consider it as spam.

Instead of creating spam, you should put up multiple online properties that discuss tips and tricks on a specific topic. If you love baking, for instance, you could put up baking recipes online through a website. You could then drive traffic to that website using search and social media marketing.

In your websites, post contents that suggest products that you use. Also, create a product review of the things you are promoting. In your reviews, you can place your affiliate links and encourage people to buy them. You will be able to build an audience using this method. At the same time, you will be able to build trust and gain rapport with this audience which will help you get more sales.

This process is not as easy as it sounds. It takes time and most people don't have the patience to keep pursuing it.

In the later chapters, we will discuss the best strategies that you can use to build your first affiliate marketing property and earn money from them.

Chapter 2 – Benefits of Starting with Affiliate Marketing

Affiliate marketing is not a get-rich-quick scheme. It requires time and patience to build a long-term and sustainable business. Most beginners usually doubt if doing this type of business is actually worth the effort.

We will discuss the many advantages of starting an affiliate marketing business in this chapter to help you decide if being an affiliate marketer really is for you.

Advantages of affiliate marketing:

- It requires little to no capital to get started

This method of earning money online requires just a small amount of capital. Some of the methods used in this book can even be implemented using only free services. For example, you can send traffic through your affiliate links using only Facebook and Instagram. You could also use your own website to do it. You can easily build one for less than $30.

- You don't need to spend time creating your own product

Product creation can take a long time. If you start a traditional business, you will need to think of a product, make prototypes of it, and test it and see how it fares in the market before you make money. Even after all this effort, there is no guarantee that you will make a profit. Before you make money, you first need to pay off the amount you spent on product creation.

Effective products usually take time to develop and sell. It requires trial and error on the part of the product creator. If you have a limited budget for product creation, the process may burn through your budget before you even reach your product launch date. There are some strategies that can be used to curve this for things like selling physical products or books on Amazon but those will not be covered in this book.

Affiliate marketing allows you to start a business with minimal risk. You do not need to risk your capital, time, and other types of resources on trial and error. Instead, you only need to focus on the most important part of the process, the sale of the product.

- You don't need years of experience to start your online business

People who have studied for many years and have had a lot of market experience and exposure create some of the most successful products and services in the world. They know what the market needs and they have the expertise to design the right products or services to meet those needs. They also have the knowledge on how to facilitate the manufacture and delivery of those products and services. They know where to find the cheapest materials and the people with the right skillset to build the products or provide services. Being able to build a successful business does not necessarily mean you have to be an expert in a given field, but experience does indeed make life easier.

With affiliate marketing, you can start a business without these prerequisites. You could learn most of the things that you need through free and premium online resources. If the processes of using these services seem complicated to you, you could also go to YouTube and check out instructions from gurus.

- You do not need to spend a lot on marketing materials or sales funnels

As an affiliate marketer, you only need to promote products and services. Even with this part of the process, you don't even need to do much because each company will create the marketing materials for you. They have a full-time marketing staff creating and testing banners, text links and even email copies for you to use. You don't even have to worry about the whole backend of each company. All you have to do is to present these marketing materials to the visitors of your own website or to the followers of your social networking accounts.

- You do not need to worry about customer service or product delivery

If you have your own business, you usually need to provide customer service to become successful. After the sale, you have to facilitate the delivery of your product or service. After this, you may still need to provide customer support to people who are having difficulties using your product.

These parts of the process are not income generating. Instead, businesses lose money when carrying out these tasks. In affiliate marketing, you no longer need to deal with these. Instead, the creators of the products and services are the ones who handle their delivery. They also provide the customer support process.

As an Internet marketer, you only need to focus on making more sales. If you do your job right, you will be able to help the people who follow your advice and the sellers of the products you promote at the same time.

Chapter 3 – Common Mistakes of Beginner Affiliate Marketers

Now that you know what affiliate marketing is and what its advantages are, let's discuss the common mistakes that beginners do when they start this type of business. You do not really see a lot of people teaching affiliate marketing free online.

The ones who say that they are teaching you free often hold back important pieces of information that are crucial to the business. Usually, they only tell you enough to get you to buy their products or the affiliate products that they are promoting. Because most people who enter this industry lack the majority of the information they need, they end up making mistakes.

Here are some of the common mistakes that beginners make:

- Thinking of affiliate marketing as a get-rich-quick scheme

Most beginners trying out affiliate marketing think that this method will make them money fast. They think that it will be as easy as building a website and driving traffic into it.

People with this type of mindset often fail to make any money. They either give up on their affiliate marketing project or lose all their capital on bad decisions. This happens when you do not have the resolve to keep doing this for the long haul.

You need to be ready to give your websites and other marketing methods at least a couple hours of your day. Your online marketing strategies will require a lot of work in the beginning. However, as you build trust with the people you attract, you will be able to sell affiliate products even though you are putting in the same amount of effort. If you keep putting in the effort, you will be able to scale your business upward.

- Being too salesy

Most beginners approach affiliate marketing like an aggressive salesman. They put up lots of call-to-actions and bright lights in their pages to highlight the product. All they talk about is the product that they are promoting. In the end, these pages never really show up in any search engines. The people who do find their website are often turned off by the salesy vibe.

You should remember that people go to the Internet, not with the intention to buy things, but to solve problems. This is the reason why many Google queries are in question form.

To be an effective affiliate marketer, you need to identify the problems that your product tries to solve and to create content that provides answers to those problems. You could start pushing your products and services when you provide tips to deal with the concerns of your customers. Make sure that the product or service that you offer to them acts as a solution to those problems.

- Making outrageous claims

Most people also make the mistake of creating too much hype for the product they are selling. In an attempt to get people's attention, they make bold claims about the product. You will see examples of this in ads of business tools that promise to help you make a million dollars. You also see health supplements that promise to make you lose ten pounds in one week.

You probably avoid ads like these. In the same way, your website visitors will also avoid them. People will think of your offer as a scam if it is presented this way. In the process, your visitors may question the authenticity of the product you are offering, hurting the image of their brand.

Instead of taking attention of visitors through outrageous claims, you should try to position yourself in the target audience's buying decision. For instance, you could create content stating the advantages and disadvantages of using your product.

Alternatively, you could create content comparing your product to other products in the market.

- Not connecting with your audience or being genuine

If you don't put out content with the true interest of helping them it will show through and people will see it clear as day. This another nail in the coffin that goes along with outrageous claims and having a salesy vibe.

This can be solved by putting out content that is truly helpful. Take time to build rapport with your audience. This is not a race it's a marathon and those who realize this and are better off than the majority of marketers. Do not ask for anything in return for a while before placing your links in front of people. Be sure to build an audience and traffic first that knows, likes, and trusts you.

- Becoming distracted and dabbling

It is common not just for beginners, to get an idea while they are still in the middle of one affiliate marketing campaign. While working on your project, you may think of other products or services to promote. If you keep pursuing all your business ideas, you could spread your time and energy too thinly and thus not fully complete anything. Your progress will be extremely slow.

If you have too many projects, you may become frustrated when you do not see results in any of them. Often, the problem stems from lack of focus on one marketing campaign or business effort. It may be more effective if you put your attention to just one campaign at a time.

If your other business ideas keep distracting you, write them down in a notebook with the intention of revisiting them at a later time. Act on them only after you are done with your current campaign. If the current campaign is not working out, you could abandon it completely and start with a new one from your notebook of ideas. But be sure to give yourself time before giving up and really ask yourself questions as to why it's not working.

15

You may be surprised as to the solutions that come up when the root cause is fully analyzed.

Coming at this with a mastery mentality can solve this. Fully devote yourself for a given time and don't even think about any other possibilities. Most importantly know that anything worth having in life is most often worth focusing on and working for as long as it aligns with how you see your future self. Does is align with your vision and purpose?

- Not tracking results

It is also a common mistake among beginners to just set up the website, Facebook pages, ads and other marketing tools and leave them alone. They start their affiliate business without a tracking tool in place. They won't be able to know where the best customers come from. You won't have anything to go off of. Because of this, they don't learn the changes that they need to make to improve the performance of their marketing tools. A saying I've heard time and time again is what gets tracked gets improved.

Tracking is the primary reason why you need your own website to attract customers. Without your own website, you will not be able to track customer behavior.

Let's say you run a product review website of fitness equipment. You created a comparison review of three fitness tools. In the process, you set up your tracking tools on the page to see which of the three tools is most popular among readers. After a month of testing, you find out that the product at the bottom of the page is most popular among buyers. To improve the click-through rate of this product, you place it at the top of the page so that it will be seen first by the buyer. Visitors who see the page are more likely to click on the affiliate link of this product because they see it first.

After a month, you check the changes on the sales of the product. While checking, you see that the change has increased the clicks on the affiliate link. You would now use the same strategy on all your other comparison reviews in the future.

- Not outsourcing and partnering with others

It is also a common mistake for most beginners to think that they can do everything by themselves. They write the entire content, do all the design factors and test out all the marketing aspect of the business. While you will save costs if you do it all by yourself, you will also burn most of your time doing things that you could let other people do.

You should let other people do the tasks that are not related to sales and marketing. As an affiliate marketer, you need to keep practicing the marketing aspect of the business. Always be willing to improve. You need to focus your time and thoughts on these aspects of the business so that you can master them over time. For the parts of the business not related to marketing and sales, you should hire other people to do them for you.

- Relying on just one source of traffic

Traffic is the life source of your business. If you have enough traffic, your only concern is on how you can monetize that traffic. However, if you do not have traffic, your sales will be severely limited and you wont' really have anyone to market to.

The biggest mistake of most affiliate marketers is relying on only one source of traffic for their online business. Google is the primary source of traffic of most websites. However, there are other places online where people spend a lot of time on. Keep thinking on where you will get your next thousand visitors. For example, you should keep your ears and eyes open for the newest social media apps. You should also keep track of the most popular websites in your niche.

When you hear of new places where you can get traffic, think of ways on how you can funnel some of the traffic from these new sources to your website. Continuously test new sources in order to see which ones boost the number of visitors to your website.

- Letting fear drive your decisions

This is a major mistake that not only affiliate marketers can make but also the average person can make on a daily basis. You may have fear about what people will think of your content or you may be self conscious getting in front of the camera for a YouTube video. I will let you know now that this will always limit you in your decision-making abilities and how you run your life on a daily basis. It most certainly will come through in the content you produce. It can also limit your potential, your outlook on life, and ultimately your success in attaining the lifestyle you dream of living.

By accepting these fears and embracing them you can ultimately free yourself. For instance I was always fearful about making books and publishing them for the world to see yet here I am writing this one. For those of you who don't want to pursue making video content because you are camera shy, just do it. The more you do this the more comfortable you will become. I was very fearful that people may not like what I have to say but does it really honestly matter? If you have something to say that really can help or be of service to at least one person out there then you would be selfish by not releasing video content. Know that this doesn't mean you that can't be successful, because you still can. You are only limiting your potential.

Once you are able to accept a certain fear you can and will overcome it by taking incredible unceasing action towards a worthy goal or purpose. Repetition is the origin and root of all mastery.

Chapter 4 – The Affiliate Marketing Fundamentals

Once you have the basics down like a website or web presence, quality content, and affiliate programs, you only then need to focus on two tasks. These are attracting traffic and promoting products or services. Sounds easy right? There are really a myriad of ways which you could approach mastering these 2 skills. In this chapter, we will get down to business and discuss how to get started.

- Attracting visitors

To become a successful affiliate marketer, you need to get the attention of a lot of Internet users. Millions of people use the Internet every day. Even if we only consider the big cities in the United States, we still get several hundred thousand people who hop on and connect to the Internet daily. Most of them are looking for ways to solve their own personal problems.

Choose a specific problem that you want to solve

Be very selective about which niche you want to choose and which problems you are looking to solve. If you are selling a video game, for example, you will find that most of the people on Facebook are not interested in downloading it on their mobile devices. If you try to market to everyone, you will mostly be ignored by the people who see your promotional materials. If you are using paid methods to attract visitors, you will end up using up your bankroll without any sales.

You are not interested in solving everyone's problems out there. Instead, as an affiliate marketer, your goal is to focus on one specific problem that many people can relate to. By focusing only on one problem, you will be able to build a following of like-minded individuals.

Before you build your website, however, you should first check if there are affiliate products related to the problem you are trying to solve. Fitness, for example, is one of the most popular niches online. You will see a lot of websites that offer affiliate programs for their own product.

On the other hand, if you teach people to dance on your website, you may not have a lot of products or services to work with. If you find that the particular niche that you have chosen does not have a lot of affiliate programs, look for other means of monetization.

If you have not started building your online marketing properties yet, you could still change your niche into something with more affiliate programs to work with. If you do change be sure that whatever you select is some thing you can be passionate about so it's easier for you to get behind the product or service.

Size up the competition

After choosing the problem that you want to solve, check if other people are already working on that problem. There are literally millions of websites out there. Each of them is trying to solve the problems of their respective visitors. Early on, you should check what other websites you would be competing with.

You can check for competition online by doing a basic Google search. You could also check the prominent online personalities in your chosen social network.

Adjust your approach to the market

Just because another website is already up, that doesn't mean that you should give up on your ideas. Instead, your competition should only guide you on the ways in which you should approach the market. Be mindful that success often leaves clues. Let's say you want to help other people by posting fashion suggestions online. You plan to create a fashion website that people can check to get wardrobe suggestions.

However, you find that there are already thousands of websites out there doing the same thing. You could still get into that niche if you approach the business from a different angle. For example, you could start by posting exclusively on YouTube because there is considerably less competition in that network. People also like to surf around to look for new videos. Your videos will show up in the suggestions and more people will discover you and your brand. You could then encourage people to click on the affiliate link in the description or go to a website that you develop in the future.

You could also approach the fashion market more effectively by narrowing the niche that you are targeting. Let's say you love dresses in particular. Instead of posting about casual wear, you could focus on promoting and selling dresses instead. This will make your brand's presence stand out because it is unique. Your audience will think of your brand every time they have an event to go to because they are looking for inspiration for a dress to wear.

Create a profile of your target audience

When attracting people to an affiliate program, you must identify the important characteristics of the buyers of the product. If you can create an accurate profile of the buyer, you will be able to target your marketing strategies to the right people. By doing so, you will lessen the effort and resources used up in promoting the product or service. You will also have a higher conversion rate because you are only showing your marketing materials to the right people.

Find out the buyers' usual buying process

Successful affiliate marketers also try to find out the buying process of the market. Let's say you are promoting a blender targeted to male athletes. You need to find out how these male athletes buy their blenders online. Do they ask their friends about it? Do they check review websites to find the best brands?

If you can learn the buying process of your target buyers, you will be able to position your marketing materials somewhere in their purchasing process.

Grab people's attention

After identifying your target market, you generally want to get their attention. We will discuss how you could go about doing this in a future chapter. For now, you should just be aware that this is the primary goal when attracting people. You need to grab people's attention with quality content and direct that attention to your affiliate link. As a reminder, it would not be a wise idea to include these links at first until you've not only got your audiences attention but their trust as well.

Most beginners make the mistake of creating content and inserting their links somewhere in a random corner where it's less noticeable. This won't exactly be helpful if you want to sell a lot of products. You want to make people look at your content or marketing material and click on it.

In YouTube, for example, you can start by creating video content that people are looking for and that is related to your product. After creating your YouTube video, don't sit idle just waiting for the views to come. You could speed the process along by marketing the video to the places online where your target audience hangs out.

For instance, you could ask permission to post on a popular Facebook group or page in your niche. This way, you will grab the attention of the people in that network. Otherwise, they will not see your video unless they somehow manage to come across it by other means.

If you have your own Facebook page and website, you could also create content related to your video and direct the users to your YouTube video where you have your affiliate link.

It is your job as an affiliate marketer to grab people's attention in a legitimate and meaningful way.

Using your personality versus being anonymous

Because of social media, it is easier than ever to connect with new followers. Many entrepreneurs are even using social media to create their own personal brand. You can also use this method to boost your affiliate marketing business.

In this process, you communicate with viewers in popular social networks like Facebook, Instagram, Twitter and YouTube. If you consistently send impactful or helpful messages that your target audience wants to hear, chances are high that you may gain a lot of followers. In this method, you are using your personality, charm, expertise, and other marketable qualities to become an influencer in your chosen niche.

Let's say, for example, you have chosen the tech niche. You create a YouTube Channel where you host a tech related show. In this show, you review products and services related to your niche. At the same time, you start a Facebook page, an Instagram account and a Twitter account to connect with a wider audience.

You create videos and share them on these platforms. People who enjoy them then start to follow you on these social networks. Over time, they become your fans. In the process, you could apply as an affiliate of some of the products and services that you review in your videos. Because of your popular status online, you may be able to get exclusive deals with the sellers. You could then, promote your affiliate link in these networks.

However, most of the readers of this book probably do not want a celebrity status to go along with their affiliate marketing business.

You could still sell affiliate products this way. Instead of creating personal YouTube videos, you use outsourced talent to voice over your videos. Instead of creating a personal brand, you create a website and pretend that there is a team of people creating the content. To keep up with the task of creating content, you also start outsourcing to sites like Upwork or ghost writing agencies. You let the brand of your website represent you in all your online marketing tools including social media. The trust of your followers in your brand will translate into sales eventually.

Countless individuals have tested both methods in the past. Both of them work in driving sales to affiliates. However, creating a personal brand seems to work faster compared to having faceless brand representation. People tend to gravitate more towards an actual face that they can match to a brand. If people see you or another familiar face using the product and talking about it they could better relate and would be more likely to leave reviews. Thus getting you more fans or visitors towards your other endeavors.

- Promoting other people's products

After successfully targeting and attracting the right types of people, you now have another task at hand. For this next step you will need to develop your promotional skills and abilities in order to convince people to click on your links. This could be reviewing or endorsing something.

Ok so you have traffic and people like your awesome content. Well in order to really be exceptional at promotion you will really need to focus on meeting the needs of your given audience. The effectiveness of your promotional efforts depends greatly on this. Once those needs are met you can convert the people you attract from visitors to customers of your affiliate marketing company. You can also try to convert people with minimal expenses on your part. This can be helpful especially if you are just starting out. Your profits from your affiliate sales will eventually outscore your total expenses for promoting products and services.

Let's say Facebook is your primary source of traffic. You will need to make people from this source click to your landing page. You need to decide what words, images or videos to use to convince them to do this. The combination of these different types of media is called a copy. You need to test different copies to refine your method. With experience, you will know the types of posts, videos, images or ads that convert well.

When it comes down to asking visitors to go to your links there are two approaches you could take. The first is called direct response marketing. This really tries to push the point home and generate an immediate response from your visitors. An example of this would be to include the link into your post or video and ask your visitor to click on it. The second strategy is called indirect marketing. With this strategy you still would promote your product or service and include an affiliate link. The difference is that you wouldn't ask for anyone to click on your link.

To refine your process, you should find a way to track the activities of the customers you attract. You need to know the number of views your copies have. You also need to track the percentage of visitors that buy. If your tracking methods are in place, you will be able to track the improvement of results with each change that you make in your copy. Successful affiliate marketers go through a cycle of testing and implementation. When they find a copy that successfully converts, they keep using it until they can create an even better copy.

Most important of all what's your current relationship like with your audience? Have you given yourself enough time to establish trust with your audience or have you been posting links left and right? Have you done your best to be genuine and does your recommendation actually mean anything? These are all very important questions to ask yourself if you are left scratching your head or are puzzled by your tracking results. You can attract traffic all day long and press hard on your promotional efforts but if you don't come off as genuine to your audience it may be an uphill battle. Try sharing your own experiences with a product or service. Why has this product or service benefited you and why will it continue to benefit others in a meaningful way if they use it? Remember your success depends upon how well you meet your respective audiences needs.

Chapter 5 – Getting Started with Affiliate Marketing

To start your affiliate marketing business, you need to sign up to a reliable network or affiliate marketing programs. In this chapter, we will discuss the process of starting out in affiliate marketing. Let's start by selecting a niche that you would enjoy promoting.

Pick a niche you are interested in

When starting out, you should approach affiliate marketing as a long-term business rather than a get-rich-quick scheme. If you think of it as a legitimate business, you wouldn't start promoting products that you haven't any interest in.

1. Create a list of your interests

Your interests and passion is the best place to start. After this chapter, find a piece of paper and write down the topics that you are most interested in. Also, include the topics related to your working experience and the topics that you want to learn.

When starting out, you will need to learn and create content about new topics. While you can outsource content creation, it's better to do some of it yourself in the beginning so that you will learn the process. It is also much cheaper to create your own content rather than rely on outsourcing services. When you start gaining income from your affiliate business you could then move towards outsourcing content creation or other activities to free up your time.

2. Find affiliate products and services related to your interests

After making a list of your interests, use the Internet to find affiliate programs related to them. If you are interested in football, for example, look for products and services online that target other football fans.

Amazon is good place to start. Most affiliate marketers start with Amazon because it is the most popular e-commerce website in the world today. If you want to promote football related products, for example, you will certainly find some of them on Amazon.

Finding an affiliate platform

You should also check if there are other products and services related to your interest outside of Amazon. To do this, search keywords related to your interest in Google with the phrase 'affiliate program' added to it.

Example:

Football merchandise affiliate program

Super Bowl tickets affiliate program

If you search these phrases in Google, you may find affiliate programs related to your interest. If your interest is broad and common enough, you will likely find something that you can promote. There are even websites like clickbank.com who will show you whole lists of products or services with affiliate programs. I've personally found and signed up for some fantastic programs on there.

Make a list of the programs available online. As a beginner, you will not be able to join some of these programs. Some advertisers only allow people with experience to start promoting their products. However, you should still take note of these offers so that you can try to apply for them in the future. In the next chapter we will cover more extensive practices on how to go about searching for programs.

3. Check the demand for the products and services

After finding offers, products or services that are compatible with your interests, it's time to check if people are looking for them online. The best free way to do this is by using the Keyword Planner from Google. By testing a keyword or phrase related to your product in the keyword planner tool, you will be able to check the approximate number of searches for the product.

Let's say you are selling a specific brand of travel backpacks and you want to know how often people search for the brand. You use Google AdWords Keyword Planner to check the numbers. It turns out, an average of 10,000 people search for the keyword of the brand every month. If we assume that 35-50% of the searchers go to the top result in Google search result pages, you should expect to get 3,500 to 5,000 visitors from this keyword alone. If we assume that your website converts are conservative 1% of your visitors, you could get around 35-50 sales affiliate sales from this keyword alone. Don't get excited yet because you need to work hard first to get that coveted top spot in Google search.

4. Check the competition

Most of the best keywords out there are already taken. If you are competing for a brand name keyword, for instance, you should expect the official website of the brand to dominate the search result pages.

Affiliate marketers often need to compete for more generic keywords and phrases. Instead of competing for the keyword 'MacBook', a more experienced affiliate marketer may try to compete for key phrases like:

'cheap laptop for sale'

'best laptops for 2016'

Just like the original keyword (MacBook), the two key phrases indicate an intent to buy by the searcher. They are also more generic, making it likely that the search results for these keywords are dominated by content websites rather than brand stores.

The best way to check if a keyword has a lot of competition is by going to Google or your search engine of choice. You could use an Incognito Mode or a second web browser that you don't normally use so that the results will not be affected by your personal information stored in the app.

In the search engine, you should use your chosen keyword or phrase in the query box. The results should show you the amount of pages and websites competing for the keywords. Avoid keywords wherein the results are dominated by big brands. You should also avoid keywords wherein the results are mostly other affiliate websites.

It is difficult to compete with other affiliates because they are also aggressive in going after the top spot. Instead of competing with other affiliates who were in the game first, look for other keywords with less competition.

5. Sign-up to your chosen platform

Before you can start your business, you will need to sign up with an affiliate program or network. You should do this before you even commit to buying a domain name or hosting package. Make sure that you can first secure the application.

Amazon Associates is probably the easiest program to sign up for. The application process takes only minutes and you only need to complete the necessary forms required by Amazon. Everything happens online so you don't need to leave your computer.

Other programs are stricter in accepting affiliates. They will ask you how you will send traffic towards their landing pages and some may even call you to ensure that you are a real person. Don't be intimidated by these processes because they happen all the time. Just answer their questions honestly and you will be accepted into the program. Most of the strict programs are just preventing scammers and black hat marketers from joining.

6. Set up your website

While selling affiliate products can still be done without a website, it is easier if you have one. One of the reasons for this is because Google is the best source of targeted traffic out there. You can only make use of the traffic that Google provides if you have your own website.

Most of the marketing strategies in this book are best done if you have a website. You can easily set up your own website using the WordPress content management system. By installing WordPress on your hosted server, you can easily modify the content of your website and the features that you want to add. You even have access to a wide variety of plugins, which help expand the functionality of your site. One very helpful plugin I have used is called Beaver Builder. This allows you to build clean and modern looking websites with all the ease of a drag and drop interface. So don't worry if you can't code in HTML, CSS, or JavaScript because tools like this completely eliminate the issue.

As an affiliate marketer, don't go crazy adding plugins to your website as you really want to limit the features available. Your visitors must be focused on your high quality and informative content and not the bells and whistles of your website. This will also help your site load quicker on different browsers and appear more responsive which can be a make or break deal for some people accessing your content, especially from mobile devices.

You should also limit the design features of your website. While you should make the design fit the taste of your visitors, do not put too many colors into it or try to be like Jackson Pollock. His paintings are great but this approach looks rather odd for a website. Really keep it clean to limit loading speed and to make a positive user experience. You can also get some great ideas from other websites in your same niche or in niches that are close to yours.

Chapter 6 – Finding Affiliate Programs in Depth

In the previous chapter we covered a basic list of what you would need to start out with affiliate marketing. In this chapter I'll briefly cover what you need to start thinking about before you begin your search. Then I'll cover the process of finding a profitable niche in depth.

Starting out

Earlier we briefly talked about finding products that you are interested in. Keeping note going forward you will want to start brainstorming at least 10 potentially profitable niches. In order to find these you will want to abide by 3 basic rules.

1. Find at least 3 potentially profitable products or services

As you search you will want to find a bare minimum of 3 products or services that you feel you could cover or have someone else cover in your given niche or market. This can really limit your options and your potential going forward if you just choose one. If for some reason one of the programs isn't working out well you have at least diversified your offerings and your chances of success will increase.

2. Have passion or at least an interest in your 10 potential niches

I can't stress this enough but make sure you have interest or a passion for whatever you decide to cover because this can really help you when times get rough and you have to keep pushing. It is much easier to push forward with something you genuinely like rather than something you just tolerate.

3. Brush off the competition

Earlier I mentioned to check the competition. However, don't ever worry or become discouraged and overwhelmed by the competition. Competition is actually a really good thing as it shows that there is a high potential for profit within a given niche or market. Take note but try not to become too obsessed about what others are doing. If you are always checking up on others you will never truly be leading in a given niche. A good quote that applies to this from Grant Cardone is "dominate in your space, don't compete in it."

How to find digital product niches

For the purposes of this section we will go to ClickBank's website. They have a huge marketplace of digital products from various companies for you to promote and sell. They do have a small selection of physical products as well if you decide this better suites what you are after. Examples of digital products could be eBooks, video training series, or even audio books. Really anything that is electronic and can be delivered over the Internet. These typically have great margins simply because they aren't physical products. The company doesn't have to go about regularly replenishing these items and there isn't any manufacturing, packing, and shipment involved.

On the homepage for ClickBank you will want to click on the affiliate marketplace tab. This will bring you to another page where you will see a lot of different categories or potential niches and markets off to the left hand side. You can really start to thumb through some of these categories to find out which products are the most popular or have a lot of affiliate marketers. You can even delve deeper and look into the sub-categories as well. I want to remind you that you won't be choosing anything just yet. This is really just to brainstorm and get a good idea of which niches are doing well.

For example let's choose the sub-category meditation under the self-help tab. This will take you a new page where you will see all of the product promotion offers. Look through these offers and see if anything stands out to you. You may find a lot of programs on chakra healing, so that could be one niche choice for instance. It's highly recommended that you click some of these offer links so you can get a better idea of what the product you would be promoting is about.

Further Criteria

Every product on clickbank.com has what's called Gravity: Shown as Grav in the stats section. This will tell you how many other affiliates are promoting a certain product and making money from it. Stay away from products that have a gravity of less than five. The reason for this is because a low number doesn't really show confidence and it's not really an indicator at this point of the programs popularity among affiliates.

You will also notice the Avg $/sale tag or the average amount per sale next to each product. I would recommend a minimum price of $10-$15. This is what you would make for an average sale as an affiliate. Taking anything less than this for product also doesn't make much sense to pursue.

Initial profit per sales or the initial commission amount is the amount you would get for the first sale of the product. The average percentage of the initial sale is also shown next to this. Some companies will offer upsells for their programs as well. The average price for this can be shown in the average rebill stat as well as a percentage estimate on the rebills.

You'll also notice certain affiliate program listings even have a website for you to go check for further information. As a reminder you want to make sure you can pick at least three products for a niche or market as this will give you an idea of how big a market could potentially be. Keep in mind this will be the core of your business. So take your time and really get a good idea for what it is you want to pursue. There is also another website called JVZoo.com which provides affiliate program offers just like ClickBank. Now that you know what to look for in terms of digital products pull out a journal, word document, or spreadsheet and write down at least 10 possible niches or markets that you have a passion or interest in that match the given criteria.

How to find physical product niches:

Here we are going to start searching for physical products we can promote on a fairly known site called Amazon. Amazon has their own affiliate program called Amazon Associates and the link to sign up is www.amazon.com/associates. With this program you can promote any product you'd like and gain a commission from it. However, the commission percentage is relatively small compared to commission on digital products. The commission can be up to 10% of the sale price of the item depending on the items category. This is still a fantastic opportunity with lots of potential.

Under the departments tab you'll want to select the full store directory. This will give you an overview of all the available categories on Amazon. You will want to go into a category that interests you. Let's pick luggage for instance because travel could be a great niche. From here you will see yet another page with choices for subcategories. The goal would be to find at least three products within any of these subcategories that are selling well. To continue with the example we will select luggage from the series of options and then select carry-on luggage on the next page that pops up.

In order to see if a product is selling well you would then click on a product listing and scroll down till you find the Amazon Best Sellers Rank metric. To the right of this you will see a number and in what category the product resides in. This number will let you know how popular an item is on Amazon in its given category. The lower the number is the more popular the item is. This number fluctuates hourly based on the number of sales purchased through the item listing. Most people recommend items with a rank of 10,000 or under for any given category. This is great general target however, these numbers are vastly different for each category and you will want to find a guide that will give you the number of estimated sales for any given item based on its rank. A company called Jungle Scout offers just such a guide. They have an estimation tool as well as a document with the full sales rank table. Using these guides' help considerably when choosing an item that is popular, has great ratings, and sells well.

Using our previous criteria browse the Amazon directory for niches and ideas. Remember the goal here is to make a list of at least 10 niches. These can be from the previous exercise. Find at least three physical products with a BSR of around 10,000 or under in the list you have chosen. If a niche you have selected has both physical and a digital choices written down or typed next to them then it's a great candidate.

Chapter 7 – Start Attracting Traffic to Your Link

As mentioned in chapter four, attracting website visitors is the next step to take once you have your website, content, and you have signed up for affiliate programs. Without traffic, you will not be able to sell anything.

What types of people do you want to attract?

After you get accepted to an affiliate network or program, study the product that you are selling. More importantly, learn the target audience of your product. Start by making a list the basic information of the target demographics. You may include the age bracket and the gender of the usual buyers of the product. Also, include the common interest of the buyers.

If there are obvious online properties where the buyers may spend their time, you should also list them down. This will make it easier for you to organize the information when you start developing your traffic gathering strategies.

When you identify your target audience, make sure that you are targeting the decision makers in the buying process. Identifying the decision makers can be tricky for most people. When selling engagement rings, for example, the product is designed for women while the marketing is targeted towards men.

The same goes for selling toys. The products are designed for kids. However, usually, the parents buy the toys for the kids. Therefore, you are targeting your marketing efforts to the parents.

Two Fundamental Attraction Methods

There are two general ways to attract people towards your affiliate links, organic and paid methods.

- The Organic Method

The organic method refers to authority and trust building strategies that create long-term relationships with visitors. With this method, you are converting visitors of your website into fans.

To make this method work, you will need a constant stream of content that your visitors find entertaining or useful. Obviously, the content that you share should always be related to the product or service that you are offering. If you already have a popular website before you start affiliate marketing, you should find affiliate products or services that are compatible with your website's theme.

You could then use various online marketing techniques to drive traffic towards your website. The most popular among these methods are social media marketing and search marketing.

After that, make your visitors subscribe to you in their network of choice. If most of your visitors come from Facebook, for instance, you could use a pop-up to encourage people to like your page. By doing so, the visitor gets to see the content you share on your Facebook page.

You could also encourage them to sign up for your email newsletters. Instead of encouraging Facebook likes, you could ask them to sign up for your free newsletter instead.

Your goal is to create a relationship with your website visitors by providing valuable content and communicating with them in your various media channels. To do this, you need to show up in your visitors' feeds or email regularly. However, you should not just email them promotional posts all the time. Instead, you should limit your promotional content to 5-10% of the content you share via email and social media.

Try to share only important content in these channels to make people go back to your website. Eventually, your visitors may develop enough trust in you to follow your advice. When this happens, they will voluntarily click on the affiliate links that you promote and start using the products or services that you recommend.

- The Paid Method

For some people, this process may seem too long. They want to try to hasten the process by using paid methods to gather traffic. Paid traffic may speed up the process if you have the right targeting tools and information. Unfortunately, most beginners are not aware of how to limit their ads only to their target audience. As a result, their ads end up being shown to people who may not be interested in their products. Their cost-per-click rises. The ad campaign ends up costing too much.

When using paid campaigns, the affiliate marketer's goal is to make the profit of the sales outscore the cost of the ads. This will be difficult to do if the cost of marketing is too high.

Refine your process

As a beginner in affiliate marketing, you should stick to the organic method for now. Build an online property that establishes trust with visitors and focuses on your chosen topic or niche. You can then test various ways of pitching your affiliate products to the visitors you attract.

With a combination of testing and implementation, you can increase the rate of conversion of visitors into buyers.

Even as a beginner, you can already start trying out paid options for advertising. You could start with simple goals like increasing your email subscribers or getting more social media followers. However, because you are just starting out, start with a small budget to minimize the risk of your online campaigns. Your goal in your early ad campaigns is to learn how to refine ad targeting.

You should also read up on how to run online marketing campaigns. The best practices for implementing these campaigns vary depending on your industry and your overall marketing strategy. For now, you could aim to practice your techniques and find the strategies that work for your own campaigns.

Where do you get traffic using the organic method?

To get traffic to click to your affiliate links, you need to know where your target audience spends most of their time online. These days, most internet users spend the majority of their time on social media apps and websites. However, some of your target audience may also be present in other web properties. Here are some of the methods you can use when researching:

- Use Google to search your niche keywords

The easiest way to learn about where most of your target audience spends most of their time is by searching a popular keyword in your niche. Let's say you want to sell travel backpacks to men. To sell this type of product, you need to advertise on online properties that attract male travelers. You could also look for mountaineering related websites. With this in mind, you can search the following keywords:

'Best travel membership sites for men'

'Best mountaineering websites for men'

If you use these key phrases on Google, you will find list articles to popular websites that may offer content related to your product. Try to find active online communities with hundreds of thousands of members. You could also look for small blogs that attract a large amount of people.

- Look at ranking websites

You could also use the data of ranking websites like Alexa.com when researching about traffic sources. You want to find the most popular online communities related to your niche. If you plan on marketing to a specific country outside of the US, use the country filter when looking for the most popular websites.

After finding these traffic sources, you should list down ways on how you can promote your own content on them. If it's a Q and A or a forum website, for example, you could aim to provide helpful answers to other people's questions. You could put links to your website in your profile or your forum signature. You could also include them in the answers if you have content in your website that is part of the solution to their questions.

Most of your answers will be crawled by Google and you may get a decent amount of traffic if you answer enough questions. Don't do this as an SEO strategy because most of these websites have a no-follow attribute to their links. Instead, just focus on three or four forums or Q and A websites where you can be a helpful member.

For starters, you can start with websites like Quora and Reddit. You could also identify forums that are specific to the niche you have chosen.

- Look inside each big social network

Most social networks and apps cannot be searched using Google. When looking for communities related to your product inside these networks, you should search from within the network. When using Facebook, for example, look for pages related to the product or service you are offering. Learning about the popular pages and groups in your chosen community will help when creating your marketing strategy later in the process.

- Getting traffic through search engine marketing

Aside from websites and apps, you should also consider search engine marketing to gain traffic for your affiliate marketing business. Search engine marketing refers to the practice of competing to reach the top of the search result pages of Google and other search engines for your selected keywords. This form of marketing requires you to accomplish certain tasks that improve the ranking of your website in your chosen search engines. The tasks that you need to do range from improving your website, creating and marketing content and interacting with other website owners.

The amount of traffic that you get from this method depends on the quality of keywords that you rank for. If the keywords that you want to rank for is extremely competitive, you may have difficulty getting traffic because other websites with better content dominate the top spot. You can use tools like Google AdWords Keyword Planner to find high traffic sales-related keywords with low competition.

Keeping people's attention

Marketers online are always fighting over the attention of internet users. After attracting your target audience to your page or your website, the next step is to make them stick around.

If you have a website, your goal is to keep your visitors returning. You can do this in multiple ways. One way is by promising them with valuable content. If people need the types of content that you offer, they will try to remember your website on their own. However, you should make it easier for them to remember your website through various subscription tools.

These days, social media seems to be the best subscription tool to keep visitors coming back. You can create a Facebook page to represent your website inside Facebook and encourage your website visitors to like your page. If they choose to do it, they may see the content that you share when they use Facebook. If they click on it, they will be directed back to your website. The same strategy could be used with Instagram, Twitter, and other social networks.

Another way to keep users coming back is by using email marketing. Most websites encourage you to subscribe to their email newsletter. This subscription is usually free. It only requires you only to enter your name and email address. In return, you will get free content straight to your email address. With emails now available in smartphones, this method is becoming even more effective.

The emails could contain anything from short articles to sales pitches. Ultimately, it invites people to go back to the website.

Kevin Ulaner

Another way to make people come back is by encouraging them to comment on your content. If they do comment, they have the option to put in their email address so that they will be notified whenever somebody replies to their comments.

Chapter 8 – Start With Your Site Structure

Search engines are smarter now than ever before. Google, for example, shows you results before you even finish typing your key phrase. Black hat methods are no longer effective to make your pages rank in Google. If there are some black hat methods that persist, it will not be long before they are made irrelevant by Google's algorithm changes.

To create a long-term search engine marketing strategy, you need to provide unique, valuable and relevant content to your target market. To do this, you will need to learn how to implement a content marketing campaign with the goal of driving traffic to affiliate links.

To drive traffic to your affiliate links, you should first decide on a structure for your website. A website is composed of web pages. These pages contain different types of content. Each of your posts and pages should have a purpose in helping you get more sales. Each post or type of content should be valuable to your visitors. Here are the types of pages that your website should contain:

Your primary sales pages

In this page, you try to convince the buyer to buy the primary product that you are promoting. It could also contain a list of the many products that you are marketing to your website visitors. However, you cannot just post affiliate links on a page and expect your visitors to click on it and buy a product on the seller's website. You need to disguise your marketing page into marketable content that your visitors find entertaining or useful.

If you are selling mountaineering backpacks, for instance, you can create an article that shows your comparison reviews of different types of backpacks. The page should contain no other outbound links other than your affiliate links. In the article, you should include different backpack brands and their descriptions. At the bottom of each article, you should include an affiliate link that leads to a page where the visitor can purchase the backpack brands being discussed.

All other pages in your website should have links that lead to your primary marketing page. If possible, you should even make this page your homepage.

Eventually, you will run out of things to say about the primary product you are promoting. At this point, you may want to add another sales page, comparing different types of products.

After talking all about backpacks, for instance, you could shift to talking about travel accessories. This page could also contain affiliate links. After creating this sales page, you should create a whole new batch of secondary pages for it.

Secondary pages

Your secondary pages refer to the pages that you create that add value to your website. Some of your secondary pages also work for social media and search engine marketing. For example, you could create news content related to your products. You could also create how-to contents that help your target audience solve a problem. The content that you create should be related to the product that you are promoting or the content of your primary sales page.

While your primary sales page is targeting its own search keyword, your other pages should aim to rank with other popular keywords related to your niche.

Some of your secondary keywords should also be entertaining articles created with social media marketing in mind. While social media traffic may not be as targeted as search traffic, you may still convert some of them.

Traffic gathering accounts

Outside of your website, you should also consider creating different accounts with the goal to lead traffic to your primary sales page. For example, you could create an Instagram account related to your product. If you are selling travel backpacks, for example, your account could be about travels. You should post content consistently to increase the number of your followers and to keep your page relevant.

Every month, you could add one promotional image instructing your followers to go to your website. This will add more traffic going to your sales page. The amount of traffic you rake into your website depends on the total number of engaged followers you have. You could also create accounts in online communities like Reddit.

Traffic Tracking Tools

After you attract your visitors in your marketing platforms, you should encourage them to click on your action link. The link you use could lead either directly to the landing page of the seller or to your own page.

If the landing page of the seller is good enough, you may lead them there directly. Most of the time, however, you will need to presell the products or services before sending them to the seller's landing page. Your primary sales page acts as your preselling platform. This page receives all the visitors that you attract through your various marketing strategies.

Marketing Tool > Sales Page > Seller's Landing Page

Aside from preselling the product, the sales page also allows you to track the activity of the buyer. If you lead the visitors directly to the landing page of the seller, you will not learn anything about the people you attract.

By using a landing page, you will be able to track the demographics and the activities of the leads. You will know where they are coming from and what their activities are before they leave. You will know the number of people who bounced or closed

Kevin Ulaner

the tab after arriving at your page. You can use WordPress plugins to track these data. You could also use free tools like Google analytics.

You can use the information from your tracking tools to adjust the contents of the sales page to manipulate the results of your campaign. The most successful affiliate marketers use A/B testing to test the success rate of different sales pages. They examine each detail of the page, replace some elements and check if the changes result to positive results.

They then, retain the changes that lead to positive results. This process allows affiliate marketers to continuously improve their conversion rates.

Chapter 9 – Strategies to Promote Affiliate Offers

Affiliate marketers fall into two general categories, content marketers, and PPC marketers.

Pay-per-Click Marketing

PPC marketers gain traffic through paid means and they usually just present lead offers to the people they attract. Their sales process looks something like this:

PPC Campaign > Sales Page > Affiliate Landing Page

They use the sales page as a preselling and a tracking tool. They use Google Analytics or other tracking software to gather information about the visitors and their activities on the page. They then, create changes and do A/B testing to improve the conversion rates of their campaign.

Most of the effort and time of this kind of marketer goes to looking for great offers to promote. Because there is no trust building process in this form of affiliate marketing, the marketer needs to find an offer that converts well. They use banner and text ads to promote the product.

They test out offers by becoming a member of Cost-Per-Action offer networks like Max Bounty. When they see an offer they like, they set up the sales page for it. If they are satisfied with the contents of the sales page, they funnel traffic towards it using PPC campaigns. They use the first campaign as a test of the effectiveness of the offer. They may start out with a modest campaign budget of $50 to $100. Using ad networks like Google AdWords and Facebook Ads, they could bring a decent amount of traffic to the offer.

If they make a profit with the first campaign, they may add budget to it to boost profits. If the profits are too small or if they end up losing money, they may stop the campaign and look for better offers to promote.

The process continues until they find an offer that they can promote for the long term. This process of promoting affiliate offers is risky because you may use up your campaign funds before finding an offer that works. Also, CPA offers are mostly short term.

However, the rewards of this form of affiliate promotion can also be big. If you do find an offer that fits with the interests of the PPC visitors that you can afford, you may get a big payday from this method.

Content Marketing

For most people, the paid method is difficult to pull off. The large amount of advertising capital needed to pull it off also makes it risky.

Most people with time to spare prefer to use the content marketing route to promote affiliate products. In the past, affiliate marketers created what they called 'micro niche websites'. These websites contain few pages and posts. The content of these websites is focused only on the product. The goal of the affiliate marketer with these websites is to make them rank using mostly black hat SEO methods.

This form of promoting affiliate products became less effective when Google improved their search algorithm. These types of websites were ranked down and were overtaken by websites with more and better content in the search engine ranking of profitable keywords.

The ones who survived the algorithm updates also improved their websites to keep their ranking. From micro-niche websites, they transformed their sites into authority websites with useful content. They also added more content and included features that improved user experience.

When creating your niche website, you want to be an authority site rather than a micro-niche site.

To create an authority niche site, you need to create and post content that covers the basics of your niche. This includes topics that are usually asked by the beginners in your niche. Start by creating posts that discuss what your niche is about. Also, discuss the common problems that people in your niche encounter.

After discussing the basics, you should begin posting your solutions to the problems you identified. In the tips and strategies you discuss, you can insert suggestions related to your affiliate product or service. You can then encourage the readers to try them.

However, your readers will not just accept your suggestions. You need to establish trust with them before they follow your advice and make purchases from your links.

Building Trust among your Website Visitors

You don't need to be an expert in your niche to establish trust with your website visitors. Many niche site builders establish authority through their content alone. You can also do this by following these tips:

- **Make your web presence look professional**

First impressions are important in online marketing. 99% of the visits in a website's first month come from new visitors. All of these visitors will judge your website the first time they see it. They look at your design and they decide whether they like your website or not. They care little about your content. Most visitors make the decision to trust you solely on the look and feel of your website.

Aside from your website, your visitors will also judge you based on your social media presence. If they discover you in Instagram for example, the will check if your pictures are good. If they don't like what they see, they will not follow you or click on the link in your bio. The same process happens in your other social media accounts.

Because of this, you should focus on making your website and other forms of online presence look professional. If you have no idea on how to do this, you could check other websites in your niche and copy the theme of their design.

Aside from the design, you could also establish a good first impression with first-time visitors through your writing. Your articles should have minimal errors. If an article is full of grammatical or spelling mistakes, people will begin to doubt its credibility.

- **Post regularly**

When a visitor first arrives at your website, he or she will look at the last date when you last posted. If they see that the website or social media page has no new content, they will assume that the owners have abandoned it. They are less likely to return to your website.

You should avoid this from happening by posting content regularly. The frequency of your post depends on the nature of your niche. If you are in the show business niche, you are expected to post content as new events happen. The same goes for sports-related content. However, if your content is not related to current events, you could limit your posting to a couple of posts per week.

- **Focus on your niche**

When you talk on your website or your social media account, you should only focus on the niche that you are a part of. Let's say you have a fitness website and a Facebook page related to it. You should not include emotional rants in your Facebook page. You should also avoid adding political or religious topics in your page unless that is what your niche is about.

People who follow you on these social networks like your page because of the niche market it represents. If your page has a lot of personal rants or negative content, your followers may unfollow you and this may affect your sales numbers.

Chapter 10 – Steps to Earn $11,000/ Month or More from Your Affiliate Marketing Business

Building a business is a lot of work. The affiliate marketing business, in particular, requires patience and dedication to make it work. In this industry, the first two months of your business is crucial. It is the time when you need to build your momentum.

If you can build your momentum at this time, you may start earning big bucks in your first six months. If done right, affiliate marketing can give you five to six figures every month.

To capitalize in the early parts of your business development, you should increase your productivity in these first two months and follow these steps:

Step 1: Review the niche you've chosen and the product you will promote

The first thing that you need to do is to review your chosen niche and make sure that it is not too difficult to penetrate. Also make sure that you have interest or passion for the given subject.

You should also make sure that the niche that you have chosen has a lot of good products to promote. The rule of thumb is to choose a niche that has many Amazon products related to it. This way, you will have many items to review and keywords to work with. You also can couple your Amazon findings with the digital product results from ClickBank and JVZoo.

Lastly, you should define the angle that you will approach the market to stand out among your competition. You should identify the defining characteristics of your website and social media presence to make you different from other websites offering similar information.

Step 2: Build a minimalist website

After choosing your niche and the products that you will promote, you should create a minimalist website. When you choose a design, make sure that it is not too taxing on the eyes. A black and white design with only one contrasting bright color should be enough to make your website look modern. Most of the successful websites today use this design model. Facebook, for instance, is a white space with blue outlines. The same is true with Twitter. You can also get great ideas or inspiration from other sites in your same niche.

These types of designs put emphasis on your images and the bold letters of your headlines. A minimalist design also makes your call-to-action buttons stand out. You could easily create this type of website using WordPress and a free or premium theme. You also have access to a free phenomenal plugin called Beaver Builder. This plugin also only functions with certain WordPress themes. So make sure before you select one that it is supported by the plugin. I have used the Tesseract theme in the past. You can find it at this link www.tesseracttheme.com.

After creating the website, start thinking of the features that you want to add. In the beginning, don't add too many features or plugins. You should also keep a minimalist mindset when selecting your features. Focus on adding only the basic social media sharing buttons. You could also add your pop-up or pop-under email sign up feature. Also, start collecting email addresses from day 1 to begin capturing leads and building a list.

Step 3: Create the primary sales page

Now that you have your website ready, you should start building your primary sales page. As discussed in earlier chapters, this page is designed to sell the product. It could be crafted in different forms.

For example, you can design it to look like an article that compares the different brands of one product. If you are promoting a hosting service, for instance, you can compare the service provider you are promoting to three other similar providers.

You could also create a page that only discusses one product. You could discuss the advantages of this product and the benefits that it delivers. The review format is popular because it has excellent SEO value. It also has the advantage of attracting search visitors that are in the later part of the buying process. The people who search for reviews have already identified the brands that they want. These people are usually in the mood for buying.

Lastly, you could also present your sales page as an all-in-one page that discusses the definition of your niche and the comparison of the different products used to solve your niche's problem. If your niche is about gardening, for instance, your sales page could be a step-by-step tutorial of how to set up a garden. In the process of explaining, you add suggestions of products. You could say something like this:

"You could use any brand of organic fertilizer for your garden but I personally recommend Brand X (add corresponding affiliate link)"

This type of sales page is even more effective in getting SEO traffic. However, it tends to attract people in various stages of the buying process. You could expect a lower conversion rate with this type of sales page.

While there are other ways to design the primary sales page, these three are the most effective in both attracting search traffic and selling products.

When designing your sales page, make sure that you answer the questions of your buyers. If you are setting up a review sales page, for instance, create a comprehensive review that provides the answer to your buyer's questions about the product. Avoid creating a short review because these usually do not do well in search engine rankings.

After setting up your sales page, you should optimize it to rank well in a primary keyword of the product and the problem that it is trying to solve. If your page is about how to set up a flower garden, you could choose from one of the following key phrases:

"Garden Design 2016"

"Organic garden design 2016"

"How to set up an organic garden"

To optimize your content, mention it or variations of it 3-5 times in your sales page. You could increase the number of times you mention it for longer posts. You should also put it in the early part of the title and the first paragraph. These three practices will often be enough to let search bots know what the page is about.

After optimizing your content, you should set up tracking tools in the page. You could do this by setting up a special Google Analytics property for it. You could also use an in-site tracking plugin as an alternative.

Important: You should make your call to action buttons in these pages more prominent that in other pages. You should also add these call-to-action buttons in various parts of your post. In long posts, for example, you should include your affiliate link in the beginning, in the middle and in the end of your post.

Step 4: Fill it up with secondary content

You should now start creating your secondary content pages. These are smaller content types that will fill up your website. In our gardening example, you could create a post about the types of plants in your garden and blog posts of your own gardening experience. You could also use your secondary posts to solve other problems that people often encounter in your niche.

You could also create posts that are more likely to be shared in social media. For instance, you could create a post about pictures of other gardens that you find beautiful and share them in social media. These type of posts are easy to create because you are merely sharing other people's content. While they don't have much SEO value, they are effective in bringing people from social networks to your website. These posts should also follow basic SEO rules. However, they should target different keywords from your primary content pages.

These posts should also contain links to your primary sales page. At the end of your secondary posts, encourage people to check out your primary sales page. You could also put links to it inside the content.

Step 5: Build your social media pages and accounts

Now that you have your website set up, it's time to send traffic to your pages. You should start by building your social media pages. In particular, you should prioritize social networks with content-sharing features. Twitter, Facebook, and LinkedIn all have these features. Instagram, Snapchat, and Pinterest are not as effective in sharing actual pages from outside the network.

To complete your accounts in these networks, you should add a profile picture of your website and add a cover photo related to it. You should also start looking for followers by joining the conversation of people around the network. As with other areas of the internet, you can gain fans by helping people get answers. You could also ask your friends and family to like your page and to encourage their friends to do the same.

In some networks, the most effective way to get noticed in the beginning is by using advertising. In Facebook, for example, you can get an initial boost of followers by getting your page advertised to users. To ensure that you get good quality followers, you should target your ads to the right people.

Step 6: Create a posting schedule and post content regularly

After setting your social media accounts up, start adding followers by participating in discussions. You could then start sharing your website content in social media to start funneling traffic.

You need to have effective post titles to get clicks. The best way to do this is to highlight the important parts of the post. Try to avoid withholding information to create mystery and curiosity. This technique is called click baiting and it is a black hat method of getting clicks. You should avoid using click-baiting techniques or you will be penalized by Facebook's algorithm.

To make sure that you always have something fresh to share with people, you should create a posting schedule. You could create the content for your website yourself or you could have it outsourced. If you have a regular job outside of affiliate marketing, you could outsource this part to free up your time. Even if you outsource the writing of content, you should still proofread it and add your own ideas to it to make them more valuable.

Step 7: Tap your other traffic sources

Your social media traffic will begin to flow in naturally, as you gain more followers and optimize your post titles.

Now, it's time to get more traffic by participating in other forums and Q and A websites related to your niche. As mentioned earlier in the book, you should try to add value to these communities by adding comprehensive answers to people's questions that are related to your niche.

As you answer questions in these communities, you should observe which of the websites bring the most traffic to your website. If Quora sends the most traffic to your website, for example, you should spend most of your time there. However, you should still keep your efforts diversified so that you are not depending only on one traffic source.

Step 8: Start sending out automated email newsletters to get people back to your website

As people begin to enter your website, you will start to capture email addresses in your popup subscription form. When you already have 30 or more people in there, you should start creating email newsletters. Your newsletters should contain one or two short articles about updates on your niche and a summary of what you added in your website. These summaries will keep them coming back to your website.

You could also set up a string of auto respond emails to new subscribers. You could create a how-to guide in your niche for example. Use the auto responder to deliver one tip from the guide each week. You can automate building email lists and auto-responding with services like Mail Chimp.

Step 9: Track progress and start optimizing website for sales

The key to making money in affiliate marketing is by controlling the behavior of the people who enter your website. Your goal is to funnel all visitors to your primary sales page. You can do this by tracking the most popular pages in your website and experiment with links to direct people to your primary sales page.

If the popular content can be associated with a product, you can also add affiliate links in them and make them a sales page. The key to success is to be subtle in encouraging people to check out the link. For instance, you could tell your visitors to check the price of the item by clicking on the link.

You should refine the design of your website to make it more successful in sending people through the affiliate link. You should experiment with all the aspects of the sales pages. The arrangement of the post is one of the aspects that you can change. You could also experiment with the colors of your links and your call-to-action buttons.

If you are satisfied with the sales of your first affiliate marketing website, you could start another one on another niche. You can successfully do this if you start outsourcing most of the maintenance tasks like content creation and design changes. By outsourcing these tasks, you can focus your own time on improving the conversion rates of your website.

If each website makes $1,000 for you each month, you only need to create 11 successful affiliate marketing websites to reach your goal. Over time, you will reach this number of successful websites.

Conclusion

Thank you again for grabbing a copy of my book!

I hope this book was able to help you learn how to start your affiliate marketing business and get you rolling with some great action steps.

I want to congratulate you for getting to this point. That means that you have read this book because you are interested and willing to really hone in on this form of passive income. You have to really be committed to the idea of having a mastery mentality. Don't succumb to the shiny object syndrome. Meaning, don't get distracted by all the other opportunities that float your way. If you really want to make this work you need to be willing to dedicate some really focused time to it and create deadlines for yourself.

Be willing and open to learn and be sure that with any of the action steps that you actually take action. Knowledge is not power, continuous action backed by ones will to learn and gain knowledge is power. Make a commitment to focus on this subject if this is what you truly desire after having read this book. What you choose to focus on is what you will attract into your life no matter what it is.

The next step is to start building your first online properties for affiliate marketing so you can start working towards building an empire, and dominating the World Wide Web.

Finally, if you enjoyed this book, then I'd like to ask you for a favor, would you be kind enough to leave a review for this book on Amazon? It'd be greatly appreciated! If you have any questions, comments, or concerns, please feel free to email me at helpfulbookideas@gmail.com.

Thank you and good luck

Made in the USA
Coppell, TX
06 October 2020

39297973R00035